To Mom!
Thank ... faithfulness & your c...

Send Me an Assist Car !!!

A Peace-Keeper and First Responders Guide to Salvation

Tommy Wright Sr.

Scripture quotations are from The Holy Bible,
English Standard Version ®
(ESV ®), copyright © 2001 by Crossway, a
publishing ministry of Good News Publishers. Used
by permission. All rights reserved.

This book is dedicated to serving all those men and women in uniform who keep us safe, bandage us when we're hurt, put out our fires and guard the unruly so that we might have peace.

Thank you to my family and friends for loving me for who I am and who I am becoming.

Special thanks to my wonderful wife Joy for putting up with all the fun and excitement that is associated with being a Cop's wife. I love you Joy!

Thank you to Tommy Jr. and Alanna for being the best blessing that God ever gave to me.

Last but not least, thank you to my Mom and Dad for raising me in Christ so that I might grow stronger in him.

Thank you to my Mother and Father in Law for raising the most wonderful, god fearing woman in the entire world!

Table of Contents

1. What the heck is this book about?
2. Why should I get to know God?
3. Who is this God you are talking about?
4. Who am I?
5. How do I accept Jesus into my heart?
6. "I am not sure about this Jesus stuff. Will you help me answer some questions that I have?"
7. How can I begin to live a Christian life and serve him?
8. Getting started on your Godly life: Issues for the First Responder.
9. Financial difficulties
10. Alcohol Abuse
11. Depression, Loneliness, Anger and Bitterness
12. Fear
13. Discouragement and Disappointment.
14. Sinfulness
15. "Respectfully submitted"

Chapter 1

What the heck is this book about?

This book is about us, the Peacekeepers, First Responders and Corrections Officers.

Every day, we are out there, on the beat, the back roads, the inner city alleyways, the slums, the mobile homes, the apartments, the million dollar houses, the hospitals, highways, jails, and prisons all across the world.

Why are we out there? Well, in short we are saving lives, protecting people, defending the innocent, pursuing the guilty, protecting property, and ensuring the laws of our great land are upheld.

We are peacekeepers and defenders of the castle. We are protectors of the innocent and the saviors of the wounded. Whether you are the cop on the beat, the paramedic on the scene, or the fireman on the ladder, we are all servants.

Let's face-it, we have the coolest jobs around. All the excitement and a paycheck too! There is a huge sense of pride in what we do.

Most of our parents and loved ones are proud of us. Your mom is always at the beauty shop telling stories of her heroic son or daughter, the Firefighter, saving the lives of the innocent children in the burning building.

Your dad is always at the local restaurant, having coffee and telling his buddies about how his "Cop" son or daughter caught the bank robbery suspect.

When your dad tells the story, you did it single handedly, but we all know that it was a collective effort.

In short, we all love what we do or we wouldn't be doing it. None of us are going to get rich in our chosen occupations, but hey, who does it for the money anyway, right?

We do it for the excitement, the thrill of the hunt, the fast cars, cool fire trucks and ambulances with all the bells and whistles.

We long for the pursuit, for the multi-car collision, the chase, the hunt, and rush of adrenaline that comes from running into a burning building.

Oh, we can say that it is for the service of mankind, and maybe it was when we first started our academy, but deep down inside, most of us knew it was to be a position of authority, excitement, and/ or control.

We wanted to be the one who everyone turns to when they need help, the shepherd guarding the flock so to speak.

Most of our days are spent doing "routine" things that our bosses make us do. You know, washing the trucks, restocking the supplies in the rig, conducting business checks, shaking hands with politicians and people who think that they are important. You know those days... shear boredom.

It is the moments of excitement we live for. We relish those moments that we have the four alarm fire, the multi-vehicle crash with injuries, the bank robbery, the pursuit, the tactical unit activation. We just cannot wait until these moments.

It is a chance for us to utilize our skills and knowledge. It is our chance to put all of our training and practice into work. It is a chance to have some excitement while serving our respective communities and its citizenry.

If all of these things sound like a lot of fun, they are! I wouldn't trade my job for anything. Oh sometimes I say I would, but deep down inside I am proud to be a Cop! Just like the rest of you are proud to be in the respective areas of your chosen service.

Despite the fact that these jobs are fun, exciting, and sometimes even rewarding, they all have downsides.

Long hours, thankless tasks, politics, time away from family, and low salaries oftentimes bring us to our emotional knees.

Let's face it. Dealing with death, despair, injury, illness, carnage and evil is our game. We see it daily. We oftentimes see people at their worst. We see them in moments of horror, wickedness, and manipulation.

We serve a people who like to manipulate and even lie to us about how they came about being in the situation that they are in. We deal with the drug addicts, drunks, sick and the silly. We deal with those who have diminished mental capacities due to substance abuse as well as those who have mental illness.

You can only see so much death and destruction before it has a profound impact on your emotions.

Although I am no expert in the subject, I think that we all suffer some emotional trauma from seeing these things. We are expected to deal with them in a "tough guy" way, never cry, and always use our dark sense of humor to cover up the huge hole that is left in our hearts because of what we have seen.

It is for these reasons that we need to cling to God now more than ever. Times are tough and the streets are hard. We hide behind alcohol use, the party life style, adultery, violence, and a tough exterior.

We often times become withdrawn from our families and spend more time with those we work with than those who really love us. Don't get me wrong, our peers love us, but not in a way that our family does, and definitely not in the same way that God does.

What we as Peace Keepers and First Responders need to do is … STOP RUNNING

FROM GOD! He is here to help us get
through our toughest of times.

God loved us so much that he sent his son to
die on a cross so that we might be saved.
Sound silly?
I know... you have to see something to believe
it, right? You're a lot like me. I got to have
some proof. I have to see some evidence.

Maybe you need to see some fire showing or
blood running before you believe that there is
an actual emergency or that something is
wrong, right?

I know your type. How do I know? I know,
because, I am you. I was one of God's children
who had gone astray, a lost sheep so to speak.

All you Cops out there will understand this
one... I was a lost sheep and the shepherd
came and found me and brought me back to
where I needed to be.

Maybe you're a cat in a tree, stuck in on a shaky limb, with no hope of climbing back down. You need a firefighter to come get his ladder and get you down. Just maybe you are that little girl, injured in an automobile accident. You need someone, like a paramedic, to come and treat your injuries.
Finally, maybe you're like that prisoner in the cell, you know the one that is always calling for help and demanding to be freed from their cell. You need a Corrections Officer to come and open the door and set you free.

We are all First Responders and we all have one thing in common. We are doing God's work. We are protecting the defenseless, righting the wrongs, tending to the sick, putting out the fires, and rescuing those who are in need of rescuing.

We are, for lack of a better term, saviors. Now I would never try to put what we do in the same context as what the Lord has done for us, but in a sense we are saving people. That is what God wants to do for you.

Before you quickly shut this book, throw it down, and say that Tommy Wright is a nut bag, I want you to hear me out. God is talking to you right now; otherwise you wouldn't have read what you've read so far.

My challenge is simple… Read on and tell me that God does not want you to accept him into your heart as your own Lord and Savior. God is willing to help you restore some peace and sanity to your life in this otherwise crazy world we live in.

God is your eternal and ultimate assist car! He is your back up when your fighting, your pumper when you need water, your bus in time of injury, and your liberator in your time of confinement.

This book is meant to give you the proper tools to learn how to call upon him to help you. It is kind of a map book, a GPS, a run card, or a guide to learning what God is all about.

I pray that through your reading of this book, you will learn just how good God is and how he can become instrumental in your life. He can help you in every way!!!

In the following chapters we will cover

- Why should I get to know God?
- Who is this God that you're talking about?
- Who am I?
- How do I accept Jesus into my heart?
- "I'm not sure about this Jesus stuff. Will you help me answer some questions that I have?"
- How can I begin to live a Christian life and serve him?
- What's next????

So, strap in, hang on, and keep your eyes open, because, this ride is about to get a little bumpy for some of you.

Chapter 2

Why should I get to know God?

Many may ask, and some may not like what I have to say, but hey, keep reading!

Do you remember your first day on the job? Most of us do. I couldn't wait. I didn't sleep the entire night before. Man, I was now a Deputy Sheriff. I was a cop ready to do battle with crime and or evil. Funny thing is, I was 22 years old, and didn't know the first thing about fighting crime, much less evil. Believe it or not, I thought that everyone respected the law like I did. Boy was I WRONG!

I started my first shift with pictures with my mom, dad, and mother and father in law. Wow, does that seem like a long time ago. I was in my tan and brown uniform, shiny boots, and all of my uniform accoutrements were perfectly placed on my blouse. Man did I look good. I couldn't wait to get out there and catch some bad guys.

Needless to say, I was a little less "bad guy catching ready" than I thought, but that is another story for another book.

The bottom line is the first night was one of the best nights of my life. I had reached my dream of becoming a Deputy Sheriff in my home county. I gained prestige with my friends, power, and on some level, a little bit of story book glory.

I was so pumped to go back to work the next shift. On my days off all I thought about was work. I read police manual after police manual. I watched all the cool cop shows and movies, and even… ready for this… listened to my walkie-talkie when I was off. I know, really rookie right? I just couldn't wait to jump back in that shiny police car and go out and enforce some laws.

I had all new friends who had great stories. Nothing was better than sitting around with some of my work buddies and drinking some beers. They would tell exciting story after exciting story. Most stories had a touch of embellishment for drama sake, but they were exciting stories. Man, the bond with those guys was strong.

Eventually, the newness wore off of the job. Make no mistake; I still love it to this day. God has really blessed me by allowing me to be part of this occupation, Sheriff's Office, and community, but it does lose a little of the magic after a while.

When the newness wore off, I started searching for something exciting, something new and fun. I got it. I had the perfect idea. Let's hang out with the boys from work a couple nights a week at the local beer joint and tell some stories? How many of you are still with me? I bet some of this has made a couple of you grin... stay tuned, it gets better.

How about this? I know, let's buy us a shiny new truck and a boat (I have done both). Then we can spend more time away from family, and more time with our buddies from work, drinking beer and telling stories about our glory days (this one too).

Is anyone getting the picture here? We are all searching for something. What we are really searching for is God. We are looking for peace, joy, and happiness. We are looking for freedom, love, and understanding.

We didn't start out looking for beers or boats or trucks, those things just happened because we were searching for happiness. Don't get me wrong, there is nothing wrong with having a boat or a truck, I am just using them as my own examples.

You see, we have this intense desire to serve the Lord, although we may not recognize it. We are always chasing something that is better than what we have right now. Many First Responders try to find happiness, peace, and joy by drinking. Others try and find it by buying new toys.

Some think that if they could just have a better looking spouse, or if they could lose a couple of pounds, then they would be happy.

I can assure you, I have looked at the bottom of many beer bottles and happiness isn't there. It is only emptiness and an upset wife at home.

It is not in a better looking spouse or even in losing some of that half price meal fat that you have put around your belly, since leaving the academy.

Happiness is in God. We pursue this happiness; but, fail to recognize that what we are actually chasing will never give us happiness. It will never give us that happiness that the Lord, our creator will give us.

I bet if you really looked at the lives of some of the most famous and rich people in the United States, you could see them running from God and chasing happiness through material things.

We may think we need to change jobs.
Maybe we think it is time to get into a
different Division or on a different truck.
Maybe a change of scenery will help.
Maybe a nicer Captain who doesn't yell so
much would help or maybe a new and exciting
assignment will do the trick. I know, maybe if
you could get promoted, then you would be
happy, right? Let me tell you, none of those
things will give you that happiness. All it will
do is give you a little something to look
forward to for a short period of time.
Eventually, even the new becomes old.

I have been really fortunate in my career to
get the chance to move around and try new
things. I have done just about all of the
exciting jobs that you can do in law
enforcement. I have come up through the
ranks and experienced triumphs and
tragedies.

None of these things satisfied my need for
happiness. They would work for a little while,
but not for very long.

As First Responders we sometimes blame everything and everyone around us for our own unhappiness. Cops, Fireman, EMS, and Corrections, we are all the same. Someone has always got to be the one responsible for whatever happens. We become very cynical and dark. When the things that we have chased no longer bring us happiness, we start looking for persons or things to blame. Maybe it isn't a person or thing that we blame. Maybe it is that we blame ourselves. Maybe we think that we are not trying hard enough. Maybe we think that we are not making the right decisions to bring joy into our lives. It could be that no matter who we want to hold accountable for our unhappiness, the real root of it is that we are actually running from it.

We are running from our back-up. We are running from God, when all we have to do is accept him as our Savior and serve him. Then we will be seeking true happiness.

Chapter 3

Who is this God you're talking about?

God is the creator of everything. He created everything out of nothing. God is the one responsible for the moon and stars, the sun and the earth. He is everything. He created everything. He is responsible for everything.

That is kind of a hard concept for any of us to believe. We have a hard time wrapping our minds around something that we can't see, can't touch, can't smell, or even hear.

Imagine getting a call to a four alarm house fire and when you get there, I am standing in the front yard yelling "FIRE". You look around but see no flame, you smell no smoke, and you feel no heat.

You are going to think that I have gone absolutely bug nuts. You are probably going to call for someone to take me to the nut house and do an involuntary committal order on me, right?

It is really hard for us to believe in something that we can't see! I will be completely honest with you, I have never seen GOD. He is there and I know he is, but he is not something tangible that we can touch. He is GOD. He just is!

This God that I am referring to is the only real God. He is a loving and just God. He loves us no matter what. Sometimes he is not very happy with us but he will always love us.

For example, you got a kid, your kid, fourteen years old, who is sneaking out of your house while you are on night shift. Your spouse is home but this kind of behavior goes undetected for months. Suddenly you are at your assigned post and you get a call from a co-worker. They got your kid and your kid has been stealing out of cars. Do you still love your kid? Of course you do and you always will.

You don't hate them but you do hate that they stole. God is a lot like that. He loves you for you, but hates when you do bad things. He will always love you. That is what I mean when I say he is a loving God.

God is also just. Take the same situation of your kid sneaking out of the house in the middle of the night and getting caught breaking into cars. We have already established that you love them still right? Are you going beat them silly? You may beat them senseless or maybe you will just ground them until they are twenty-five. You still love them just not what they have done.

The point is that you still love them but you are going to punish them for their wrong-doings. God is the parent and you are the child. He still loves you but might give you a small spanking for your misdoings, but he will help you through those consequences.

Please don't misinterpret the previous statement, as I do not prescribe to the retribution theory, I am just trying to make a point. Bad things do happen to good people. He is not going to love you any less if you make a mistake, and he is certainly not going to "smite" you for making a mistake. God is grace and mercy.

Before I go very far with those two terms, let's define them in simple terms. Grace is receiving something that you don't deserve and mercy is not receiving something that you deserve.

In the old days, God would just rip you a new one for messing up and that was the end of it and you. That changed though. Over time God displayed his mercy and his grace by sending his Son to earth in the form of a man. That man was Jesus and he was perfect. Jesus was sent to earth in human form to die for our sins.

You ever watch any of those old movies about biblical days? You see where they cut up a lamb and burn it as an offering to God?

Jesus was that sacrificial lamb. Jesus died upon the cross so that we might live. That is pretty cool when you think about it. Someone died for us so that we might live.

Just like those on the job who died fighting the fire, trying to pull the crash victim from the mangled wreck, or trying to protect the weak against the predator. Jesus was that cop, that firefighter, that paramedic, that corrections officer who died in the line of duty. The difference is, he died willingly, not accidently or by some strange occurrence. He knew that he was to die so that we might be saved.Jesus died for us even though we didn't deserve it. He died so that we might have ever lasting life. That is a sacrifice that most of us who have been on the job for a while have seen made. We have all had co-workers killed and buried. It hurts us and our families.

Every shift, watch, or assignment that we go out on, the possibility exists that we may give our life for the service of someone else.

That is what Jesus did for us. He died for us. He is our assist car and all we have to do is pick up that metaphoric radio mic and ask for his assistance.

The point I am trying to make is that God showed mercy on us by not kicking our butts for our disobedience and sin even though we deserved it. He also showed grace to us by sending his son to die on the cross so that we might have everlasting life in heaven even though we didn't deserve it.

Chapter 4

Who am I?

You are one of God's children. You are the one that he has chosen to have a relationship with.

He created and designed us after his own image (No, God is not ugly like your buddy's wife). He created you out of nothing for the simple purpose of having a strong personal relationship with you. That is it. That is why you are here.

You may argue that you are a Cop, Firefighter, Paramedic, or Corrections Officer. You may even argue that you are a father, mother, aunt, uncle, cousin and so on. Although all of those may be true, those are not who you are. You are one of Gods children. That is it. That is the bottom line.

We are God's creation plain and simple. When he first created us he gave us some rules, just one actually. That rule was to not eat from some silly tree in the Garden of Eden.

If you are like me, when someone tells you not to do something, you think that that they are telling you not to do it because they don't want you to have any fun. You know what I mean. Your boss tells you that you shouldn't do something; they are just trying to be a stick in the mud. After all what do they know anyway, right?

Well, that is kind of how Adam and Eve fell. They didn't listen to God's only rule and "POW", they were naked and ashamed.

We are just like them in the sense that God is telling us how to behave and what he expects of us; but, every day we show him that we know just a little more than he does. At least, we think we are showing him that, but in the end, he is just sitting up in heaven, smiling, and waiting to help you pick your silly butt off of the ground when whatever it is that you're doing goes poorly for you.

As his creation, we have shown him time after time after time, that we think that we are smarter. We reject God and his commandments so that we might have a little fun.

First Responders are a breed all of their own. We are probably worse than any other sub-culture of people when it comes to this kind of rebellion.

After all, we are adrenaline junkies; Type A, assertive personalities that like to be in charge. If we weren't this way, we probably couldn't do the job we do.

Imagine a scared little girl with a fire hose in her hand and a trapped victim on the fourth floor of an apartment building that is on fire. The victim is screaming for help. If we weren't wired this way we probably would have the same fearful reaction as that little girl holding the hose. We would do nothing, just stand there and cry

I think God has a special love for First Responders and I think that he understands the demands of the job that we do. That is why he is so merciful.

We spend so much time trying to please ourselves and obtain wealth, power, notoriety, rank, the upper hand, and material items that we never quite find the time to devote to his service. God wants us to know, love, and serve Him, but again we chase after happiness elsewhere. We substitute the love of things for the love of God which is a dangerous proposal. Remember, God built us to worship and serve him.

If we are living on our own and not serving God, we are serving something other than him. Maybe it is ourselves, or our jobs that we are serving. We might be serving our own selfish pursuits like working a second job so that we can buy that lake house, or the hunting gear that we want. It could be that we are serving our own lustful desires of impressing the ladies or the gentlemen. Who knows?

All we do know is that if you are not serving him you are serving another god. You are serving a god that you will eventually lose passion for. You will be serving a god that will not provide long term satisfaction, and certainly will not provide eternal life.

Chapter 5

How do I accept Jesus into my heart?

O.k.… I got to ask. Is God talking to you yet? If you say no, I am going to slam my hands on the table in front of you and start screaming, "LIAR", just like in Cop movies. I hope you know that kind of interview technique doesn't really work.

You know, salvation is a pretty simple process. God doesn't ask a lot from his creation. He wants us to admit we are sinners, turn away from the sin, and believe that he is God and that he sent his Son to die on the cross for your sins. The final two things that we have to do for salvation is ask him to be our Lord and Savior and to come into our hearts, and follow through with your commitment to him.

For all of the cops in the room, and just so we make it as simple as we can for you, I am going to break each salvation step down for you. Somewhere there is a firefighter laughing right now and saying "That's right, stupid cops".

We must first believe that we are sinners and identify the sinful things in our lives. This may not be so easy to do for someone who didn't grow up in a church.

For the purposes of this book, let's just say that sin is doing things that God would not want you to do. Now, you might have a different interpretation of what behaviors that you think God is ok with versus what behaviors that I think he is ok with. That is ok for now. I don't really want to get into any kind of religious or theological debate with anyone about this right now.

<u>Sin is simply this:</u>

- Not following God's rules.
- Living as our own boss rather than allowing God to be our master.

- Worshipping the wrong things. *Things that aren't GOD.*

<u>First</u>, you must repent. Believe and admit to God that you are a sinner. You have to admit that you are "guilty as charged" with breaking God's rules that he has set for your behavior.

<u>Second</u>, you must seek his forgiveness. As I previously stated He is a gracious and merciful God.

He has displayed these things by not kicking the crap out of you for some of the bone headed things that you have done. Things you deserved to be beat up for, God has not done it. He has shown you mercy.

He has also displayed his grace by allowing his son, Jesus, to die on the cross for our sins. His Son, in cop and corrections terms, served your death sentence for your crimes that you were convicted of and sentenced for. Pretty amazing stuff, huh?

We have to ask God to forgive us of the things that we have done wrong. It is called repentance. In order for God to come into our hearts we must repent and turn away from those sinful ways. We must take a different path. You must be willing to change your life and display willingness to serve and worship God.

Third, you must believe in him. You must believe that he is God, a sovereign God, who is all powerful. He is the ONLY real God.

You must have faith and trust in him. You must now rely on God and not the other things that you have relied on in the past to help make you happy. You must relinquish your own personal feeling, beliefs, and fears to him. Faith in Him and changing your trust to Him and not yourself is a good way to surrender.

This is hard for First Responders. First, it is hard because God is something that you cannot see.

The notion of us surrendering to something that we cannot see, touch, or smell is almost unheard of.
We are a suspicious bunch and are always seeking physical proof of things. We need to have something in front of us to believe in it.

God is real and this is a hard step for you, I know, but believe me when I say, you can do it. God is good and he will bring you through your suspicion and will open your eyes to his love.

The <u>fourth</u> step is easy. You must ask him to come into your heart and life. This is the total surrender portion that is very important.

There are many different prayers out there that you can use, but it doesn't need to be complicated. If you want, I can help you by providing a guideline prayer that will help you ask Jesus into your heart.

Here it is:

God, I am a sinner. I am flawed and imperfect. I have not always done the right things in your eyes.

I have seen some bad things over the years. I have seen people in some of their most horrible and sinful times.

I have been a good servant of my community as a First Responder, but have not led the life that you have wanted me to be living.

I believe that you sent your Son, Jesus Christ, to the world. I know you sent him to die on the cross for my sins so that I might live in your kingdom forever.

I now surrender to you and ask you to come into my heart and life so that I may forever worship you.

Please forgive me of my sins and make me a servant of you so that I might have ever lasting life.

Lord I am turning away from my old life and starting a new one that will revolve around serving you.

Jesus, please fill me with your spirit and give me the courage, faith, commitment, and help so that I may live a life that is good and pleasing in your eyes.

Thank you for your love, mercy, and grace.

Amen.

See how easy that was? Feel better? I am telling you that you are going to start feeling better and looking at the world in a whole new way. God is good to us. He loves First Responders. I know that you are going to be a warrior for him. You are going to live a life that will exemplify him and make him proud.

This is not always going to be easy though. You're going to take a little ribbing from your work Buddies. Remember, they are searching for some of the same things that you were. Be an instrument of his love and witness to them. Tell them about his goodness and grace.

In the next chapter, for those doubters, we will talk about those of you who didn't give your hearts and life to the Lord.

No, this next chapter won't be a chapter about fire and brimstone, a lake of fire and damnation. It won't condemn you for not asking Jesus to help you. It will address some of the issues that you may have with salvation. It will be a chapter that answers the question; "I'm not sure about this Jesus stuff. Will you help me answer some questions that I have?"

If you have accepted Jesus into your heart, go ahead and read the next chapter. The next chapter will give you some information to use to when trying to lead your buddies to salvation. They may have some of the same questions that you did.

For those of you that accepted Jesus, Chapter 7 will talk about what to do next. Sorry we have to do it this way, but I have to take care of those who are being hard headed first. You know who those are. These are the tough ones, the ones who will resist the most.

Have faith because we are going to get them too. I just have to explain it to them again.

Chapter 6

"I'm not sure about this Jesus stuff. Will you help me answer some questions that I have?"

Well, you have made it through five chapters already. I think that means that God is dealing with you, but you might be a little scared or even have apprehensions about making a commitment.

I will tell you that I understand your reservations about it. I sure had a lot of reservations of my own. Most of my reservations were about peer pressure and not wanting to give up some of the fun things in my life like partying with the boys from work and drinking beer.

I worried what my friends would think and how much they would make fun of me. I worried that my peers would doubt my commitment to Christ and that they would try to place temptations in my path so that I might stray.

I didn't worry about what my bosses would say because they are all good Christian men and women. They are solid and sound, so this wasn't a big problem for me, but it might be for you.

I also worried about what my family would say. My wife and I had established a life far outside of Christ's expectations. We weren't bad people but we didn't live a life that represented God's teachings.

One thing that I failed to mention earlier was that she and I grew up in church. We actually met at Kids Church Camp at the Lake of the Ozarks during the summer of 1982. Yes, for those of you rookies that are reading this book, I did say 1982. Yes I am old, but I also have maturity, experience and RANK, so watch what you say!

My wife and I grew up in humble, God fearing homes. We both have parents who are still married, and still love God. I will tell you that when I was a kid and the church doors were open, we were there. It didn't matter if I wanted to go, I was going. Every Sunday morning, Sunday night, Monday night, Wednesday night, and heaven help you if a revival was going on. I remember one revival at our church that was supposed to be like three days; but, it lasted like a month, every night for an entire month. As a young, energetic, and enthusiastic little boy, going to church that often was a bit much, but I lived. It was good for me whether I wanted to admit it or not. Thank you Mom and Dad for making me go to church.

My wife and I enjoyed hanging out with friends, going to the winery, bar-b-que and drinking beers with friends, and things like that. We weren't out robbing banks or stealing cars, but we weren't living a Godly life. We had some worldly fun, but we were still searching. I feared that maybe my wife wasn't ready to go back to church.

I feared that maybe my kids would think that Dad had gone crazy or grown weak in his old age.

I worried about those from other agencies that I had hung out with, or how I was now going to be perceived by my peers as a Jesus freak.

I feared what it would cost me financially, socially, and emotionally. I am sure that some of you have some of the same reservations.

Maybe you don't understand Christianity or maybe you have only seen that television preacher begging for money and telling people they are going to hell.

You might have some problems with your beliefs that you have had for a long time. Maybe those beliefs don't match up with what I have said.

Maybe you don't understand the concepts of faith, Jesus, his death and resurrection, sin, or other matters such as these.

Finally, maybe you don't completely understand Christianity and the Bible. Maybe you just cannot figure out what the bible is saying.

This chapter is going to address all of those things. There is no way that I could possibly cover every possible problem, reservation, or lack of understanding that everyone may have with Christianity and salvation. I am going to give it a try though.

Let's go on and see if I can convince you that you need Jesus in your life. Here we go!

First of all, let's take one question, or issue at a time. I know that many of you are worried about what your friends and co-workers are going to say. This is a very real concern for First Responders.

We are a rough and tumble group. We have no fear, are in charge of every vital situation, and like it or not, we care what our co-workers think about us. Our jobs are about **PRIDE, COURAGE, LOYALTY, COMMITMENT, SACRIFICE, and BROTHERHOOD or SISTERHOOD.**

More importantly, we develop large egos that are fueled by our power, authority, and esteem. We are critical of our peers and know that they are critical of us. This is true whether you are on duty or off duty. It doesn't matter, because once you strap on that badge and uniform, you are forever changed.

You might be the brand new Paramedic who recently discovered that hanging out with others paramedics when your off duty is fun. You are now a lifesaving instrument. You are revered by the community. You are different from other civilians who don't understand what you are going through while you are at work.

You might even be an old Corrections Officer, hardened by years of con-men antics, and dealing with some of the darkest people on earth. You have grown set in your ways. You cuss, you drink, and you hang out with co-workers in social settings who do the same things that you do. Heck, who knows, maybe you fight and chase the opposite sex all the time. Maybe you don't do any of the above things, but you still will be concerned with how your salvation will be received by your peers.

The bottom line is simply this... You cannot go another day without salvation because you never know when your final shift will be. You must act now. I am not saying that today is the last day of the world, what I am saying is that today could be your last day. That is the hard and fast truth. We never know when it will be our time. We never know when some bad guy or girl will take our life. This is true in every First Responder occupation there is. A few years ago, in the St. Louis Missouri area, a car fire call went out in the early morning hours.

When the Fire Trucks and cops arrived, a man across the street started shooting with a high powered rifle. The disturbed man was able to shoot two police officers and a firefighter. That firefighter died on the scene. The suspect set his own home on fire and later was found dead in the burned out rubble.

The point that I am making with this illustration is that you just never know when you will die. I am sure that any of those First Responders involved in that shooting incident felt that the call they were receiving for a vehicle fire was going to be their last.

I guess the real issue is what is the social cost of salvation for you, the First Responder? This is a hard question to answer because each of us has a different situation; but, overall I would say that the cost is really nothing.

"Nothing, you say?" What about when none of my friends will call me, you ask. What about when they snicker and tell Jesus jokes? How about not being able to go hang out with them after work? These are all real concerns for us. We want to be looked upon in high esteem by our peers. We want them to like us, because after all we are different from all other people. We need them to accept us because they know how we feel and what we go through daily.

In short, Jesus suffered at the hands of people. He was mocked, spat upon, and later died as a result of non-believers. This was all part of God's bigger plan, a plan that would result in our eternal life and the forgiveness of our sins.

If you find yourself ostracized by your co-workers, use it as a tool to help lead them to salvation. I can tell you for sure that when the chips are down for them personally, they will come to you for prayer. So what if you don't get to go hang out at the local watering hole and act foolish. The friends that you have will still be your friends. The friends that you thought you had who will make fun of you for your new Christianity, well; they were never your friends to start with. A true friend will still care for you despite your new "Jesus Freak" lifestyle. You're not going to be missing much I can assure you. I am not!

I know that this is not an easy decision for you to make. It wasn't for me, and I grew up in church. I struggled with it for a long time and can tell you that most of my reservation was the social cost.

I get a little razzing from the guys, and you will too. They will kid you about snake charming at your church, tell you your church is creepy, and maybe even come up and grab your head and "cast out the demons". That is all a true story, all that has happened to me recently. I love the men and women that I work with. They are some of the most caring, hard working, and dedicated individuals that I have ever been around. They are also some of the most callous, malicious, and mean spirited people when it comes to trying to aggravate their co-workers. I mean to tell you that when they find something out that may hurt your feelings, well, it is like a blood in the water that is filled with sharks. Everyone wants to take a well intended shot at you.

Now I say this, but those of you reading this are probably First Responders yourselves, so you understand. Although we may be mean to each other, we would also lay down our life for a fellow First Responder. We would do so WITHOUT HESITATION.

There is a social cost associated with salvation, but the cost is minimal compared to dying without knowing Christ as your personal Savior. With God's help you can weather these storms.

Allow God to make you an instrument of his message and promise. I will tell you that the other First Responders are searching for happiness just like you. Let them know that there is happiness in God's work and way of life.

During the initial times of my transition, I was worried what my wife and kids might think, you know, Dad going to church and all. Actually, I take that back, I was worried, but my wife wasn't. It seems that God was dealing with her too. We both knew where we needed to be, but had been trying to pursue happiness through other non-Christian outlets. She actually encouraged me to go back to church. When I mentioned it to her, she was on board from the start.

My daughter was too. She gladly went to church with us and still does to this day. I am so proud of her. She is a really solid teenage girl with a heart of gold. She is beautiful, smart, and very kind. She reminds me of her mother. Our son is a great kid. He is polite, handsome, and charming. He is a real heart throb of all the young girls.

I wondered what my kids would think about their "fun/cool dad" going to church. No more drunken bashes out in the backyard pool. No more bon-fires and beers with dads NARC buddies. Dad was toned down. I couldn't help but try and anticipate how they were going to react to it.

Our son is a United States Marine and we hadn't seen him in some time. He came home on pre-deployment leave several months after we had given our hearts back to the Lord. The amazing thing was it that he was very receptive as well. We knew that he had given his heart to the Lord during basic training at MCRD San Diego. Now he isn't always an angel, but he is a good kid and has accepted Jesus into his heart.

Just a side note and a small bit of fatherly pride and worry, he is currently serving in Afghanistan as an infantryman with a bomb sniffing dog. His mother and I pray and worry daily, but have turned it all over to the Lord. I think that is the only way she and I have any peace right now.

For me, this became the opportunity for me to become the spiritual leader of our family. God intended this when he created me and now it was time for me to take up that obligation and serve him. What a great decision it was too! Thanks God, I needed it.

As far as a monetary cost, well, that is a topic debated by many. We First Responders don't make the most money in the world. In fact all of us are underpaid for the type of work we do. We are underpaid and overworked.

Salvation is free. That is why Jesus died on the cross for our sins. You don't have to buy a ticket to get into heaven. You don't have to give a bunch of money to the local church to get to heaven. You live according to God's word, believe, accept him and surrender your life to him. That is how you get to heaven.

Many of you will find the preachers, evangelists, and the ministers on television encouraging you to send money. Sending them money will not buy you a place in line outside the Heavenly Gates. I believe that you must tithe according to the bible.

God wants and commands that you help support the church. It is your duty.

Tithe means ten percent, but starting off, I wouldn't so much concern your selves with the financial cost because salvation is free.

I am going to say this, and some may get mad, but I don't care, because it is true. Now, if a preacher is constantly asking for money and links money with salvation... RUN. This is not where you need to be as a Christian. God didn't say that and it isn't true.

Some of you may not understand such concepts as faith, salvation, or even who Jesus is. You may not know what it means to be a Christian. I am no theological scholar, and can only answer these questions from the standpoint of a lay person who believes in Jesus and salvation. Remember, I am just a dumb cop.

Don't expect this to be too fancy, just a straight up explanation from a guy just like you.

First, we have already talked about who Jesus is. He is God's only son. He was sent from heaven to the earth to teach, preach, and later die for no other reason than to be a sacrificial lamb. He was God in human form.

Remember we talked about sacrificing lambs early in the book and how in the olden days this was how sins were cleansed. Sometimes people were even called to sacrifice their children to cleanse sin. No joke, that is true. Jesus was God's sacrifice so that we may live in eternity with him forever.

Faith is the practice of believing in something that you cannot see. Faith is trusting in something that isn't tangible, something that you cannot hold in your hand. It is hard for us to do that when our entire work lives revolve around facts, circumstances, evidence, and physical signs.

Whether you're the cop on the beat or the paramedic in the truck, we must be able to see it to believe it. This is not true with faith. We must believe the bible and everything that it says. Then and only then can we have faith.

Sin is a violation of law, mainly God's law. It is rebelling against his wishes and not doing as we are commanded. For us cops that is an easy concept to grasp. When someone violates the law, they have committed a crime and sinned against our societies standards. When we fail to obey God's laws we have committed a crime. We have failed to live by his message and orders. Now, violating human law can result in incarceration, but violating God's laws without repentance will result in a trip straight down to hell where you can bet that it is a little hotter and more humid than an August day in St. Louis Missouri.

Salvation is a difficult concept to grasp. The thought of someone saving us may be a difficult pill to swallow. After all, we are tough and don't need anyone to help us. We are in charge of most situations. We are the shepherds, the saviors, the healers, and the gate keepers. We don't need help, right? Wrong.

In today's troubled times we need help more than ever. Violence is rising, the streets more dangerous, and people are more desperate. The economy is plummeting; politicians are telling bigger lies and lining their pockets with more of our money. Jobs are in the toilet and people are living on the streets. We need saving.

God wants to save us. Maybe he will save us from a bad situation, or even save us from our own devices. He sent his son to die so that we might live.

Salvation is the act of saving something, usually associated with people or lives. God is knocking on your hearts door. You know he is or you wouldn't be fifty or so pages into this book. You are searching for freedom, happiness, love, and commitment. Jesus offers all of those and more.

Christianity is living a Christ-like life. It is worth a try. Obviously, if you weren't a little curious, you wouldn't have picked up this book. If you don't like it, go back to being the same old you. I can tell you that if you try it, God is going to move you like no other person or thing has ever moved you before. You will gain peace and understanding.

You will become a better person through God's leadership and direction.

I hope some of these rants have helped you to understand God's message and the importance of salvation. God is dealing with you in the most important way of your life right now. Accept him and believe that he died on the cross for you. You need to become the spiritual center for your family. You will become a better First Responder, husband, wife, mother, father, sister, brother, and so on and so forth.

This is a call for you to stop running from God and chasing pursuits of the flesh. God is good and has promised you life in heaven, all you have to do is admit you are a sinner, repent and ask forgiveness of your sins, ask him to come into your heart, and follow him.

Take a moment and reflect on this chapter. Realize that everything in the bible is true. Jesus really did die for us so that we could have salvation. Accept him as your savior. Do it right now, where you are at.

I realize that this may be a bit redundant, but I feel compelled to put the salvation prayer into this book again. Especially, since you are the hard head that I had to write this chapter for.

Here it is; Remember God loves you and that he gave his only son so that you might have life eternal.

God, I am a sinner. I am flawed and imperfect. I have not always done the right things in your eyes.

I have seen some bad things over the years. I have seen people in some of their most horrible and sinful times.

I have been a good servant of my community as a First Responder, but have not led the life that you have wanted me to be living.
I believe that you sent your son, Jesus Christ, to the world. I know you sent him to die on the cross for my sins so that I might live in your kingdom forever.

I now surrender to you and ask you to come into my heart and life so that I may forever worship you.

Please forgive me of my sins and make me a servant of you so that I might have ever lasting life.

Lord I am turning away from my old life and starting a new one that will revolve around serving you.

Jesus, please fill me with your spirit and give me the courage, faith, commitment, and help so that I may live a life that is good and pleasing in your eyes.

Thank you for your love, mercy, and grace.

Amen.

Now, don't you feel better? I think you do, if you prayed that prayer. If you didn't pray and ask God to become your savior, I encourage you to keep reading.

You may have other issues or problems with Christianity that I may address in later chapters of this book.

If you read this entire book and have not accepted Jesus as your savior, but feel like you are still searching, maybe you should contact your department's chaplain. Your chaplain may be able to help you work through some theological issues that you have with Christianity. They may be able to answer questions that I have failed to address.

If you don't have a department chaplain, maybe you could stop by one of the local Christian churches. I am sure that the pastor of one of these churches can help you. The bottom line is that I am simply a layman. I am not a minister, a preacher, teacher, theologian, or evangelist. I am just a cop who finally wised up and surrendered to Jesus. If I can do it and understand it, then you will also be able to accept Jesus as your savior.

Chapter 7

How can I begin to live a Christian life and serve him?

Well, you have made it. You have either accepted Jesus into your heart, made him your master, or you are reading the rest of this book to see what kind of crazy stuff I am going to say next. Either way, I am good with your reading. Keep going.

One of the next steps in your walk with God is to get a Bible. I don't really care what kind of Bible you get. There are a number of them out there to choose from. Go to your local bookstore and ask them. Get the easiest one for you to understand. I am a little thick headed so I prefer the English Standard Version. This is a personal preference and you might have to shop around for a version that suites your needs. I will tell you that you have some die- hard people out there that will claim that you have to read from one version or the other. Let's just take a look at it from this perspective.

Several hours ago you were not a Christian and you weren't reading the Bible anyway. If you are reading it now you are one million times better off than you were hours ago. Enough said about that.

Through reading the Bible, you will gain insight into your creation and the creation of everything. You will learn about God's people, where they were, where they came from, what happened to them, and how we came to have Jesus as their savior. Trust me, it is a great book filled with all kinds of wisdom and knowledge. By reading the Bible you will understand what the walk with God is all about. You will know what your actions are supposed to be and it will provide you with that satisfaction that you have been looking for. God wants you to read his word. God is the word. The Bible was written by many different authors, all of which were either told, by God, what to write, or they received some sort of spiritual and Godly verbal direction on what to write. Either way, it is pretty cool.

Pray. Prayer is communication with God. It is our way of keeping our lives on the right track with God. If you are going to follow Jesus, you have to pray. Prayer can get you through the day. It can get you past some of your most troubling of times. It can help you draw closer to him and make your walk with him much easier.

When you're done praying, pray some more! I can't stress this part enough. As a First Responder, you have to have adequate communications with your bosses, peers, and dispatch. If you don't, things go completely crazy. God knows this and wants to hear from you daily.

Don't just ask for a million dollars when you pray. Thank him for what you have and what opportunities have been given to you and your family. Thank him for his goodness and mercy. Pray for God to lead you while you perform your duties. Pray for God to give you the strength to be the spiritual leader of your home. Pray that God would help you to provide for your family. Pray that God will help deliver you from your bad habits. Pray that God will let you be his instrument of love and peace in a violent world.

You can talk to God anywhere, anyway, at anytime. He never sleeps, takes a vacation, or goes away. He is the ultimate First Responder and the first assist car you should seek when times get tough.

Go to church. This is really important; but, I don't think that you have to be there every time the doors are open. God wants you to meet and celebrate Christian living with other believers. This doesn't mean that you have to be part of every church committee, be a deacon, or even lead the song and praise service on Sundays. What this means is that God knows that you need to be around other Christians.

Through seeking Christian fellowship, you will draw stronger in your faith and your walk with God will be more productive. Again, I am not saying that you have to go every Sunday, but you do need to be around other believers.

Now comes the question, what kind of church should I go to? That is a good question and I am not going to specifically answer it. Well I am not going to answer that because there are so many different denomination, preachers, belief systems, and rules that only you can answer this.

Here is what I would tell you to look for. First, look for a church that believes that God is the only God and is a sovereign God. That he is the creator and ruler of all the earth and of all things. He is all powerful and all knowing. This church will be a Bible believing and teaching church. There are churches of all kinds, big ones, little ones, and everything in between. You need to go where the good Lord leads you.

Maybe, there is a Bible believing church next to the Station. Go there. Maybe you will find some new friend during your initial walk with God who can direct you where to go.

Let me warn you, these churches are filled with sinners! Yep, that is right, filled with sinners. They are filled with people who judge the drunkard on Sunday morning, but have a little nip of wine with Saturday night's dinner. They are filled with adulterers, liars, cheats, drunks, dope heads, and all other kinds of unimaginable turds in the punch bowls. You know what? That is where those people are supposed to be.

God loves everyone, especially the sinner. Remember, he sent his son to die on the cross, so that the SINNER might be saved.

You wouldn't believe the number of times that I used the argument that I didn't go to church because it was filled with hypocrites. Well yeah! DUH! That is where they are supposed to be. We are all hypocrites.

Do you ever get angry and yell at someone even though they don't deserve it, but when your kids do it, then it is a violation of your rules? Hypocrite! Do you ever write a ticket for speeding and then later find yourself doing ten over going to lunch? Hypocrite!

The point that I am attempting to make is that we are all sinners. We all make mistakes both big and small. We all judge people and then sometimes turn around and do the same things that we were judging them about.

Don't get too stoked on the hypocrisy that you find in churches. It is everywhere you look, not just in churches. At least the people in church are attempting to live right and more than likely asking for forgiveness. We are all sinners and we all need to be in church. It will provide you with encouragement, strength, and a stronger commitment to walk with the Lord.

So, to recap this chapter; because, I think we need to review it so that it sinks in, let's take a look at what we talked about.

In order to live a Christian life, we must:

- Admit our sins
- Ask God to forgive us of those sins
- Ask him to come into our hearts
- Serve him
- Read the Bible
- Go to church

That all sounds pretty easy. The ball is in your court. God bless you on your endeavor to live a Christian life. You will find that it will be the best thing that has ever happened to you and more exciting that any fire, pursuit, prison riot, or industrial accident that you have ever worked.

Remember that Jesus is always there. He is there on a 24/7 shift. His unit is always gassed up and ready to go. All you have to do is pray and cry out for help and he will come running to your rescue.

Remember…

God is your ultimate assist car.

Chapter 8

**Getting started on your Godly life:
Issues for the First Responder and how the
Bible relates to them.**

Next, I want to take a little time and discuss some topics that you may encounter when it comes to living the Christian life as a First Responder.

 I think I find this important to discuss as we as Peace Keeper and First Responders are completely different than any other group of peoples on this planet. We have a different outlook on life, see more horrific things, and see the worst sides of people that are imaginable.

 The Christian life isn't easy. If it was everyone would do it. Most people are too lazy and undisciplined to live this life that will bring them life forever.

I don't have all the answers and would never claim to. I do have a book that has all the answers in it. It is called the Bible, God's word. God is the Bible. It is his preaching, teaching, and commandments.

The Bible is an authoritative history book designed to help his children navigate in their time of need and in their time of thanksgiving.

Over the next several chapters we will talk about some of this Jesus stuff, mostly what the Bible says and how it impacts us as First Responders. So, if you have a Bible, take it out and follow along. If you don't, just continue reading and I will do my best to help you understand the context of the Biblical passages.

I will be utilizing the English Standard Version Bible for any scriptural references in these next few segments.

So sit back and enjoy this new ride we are about to take. It will help you to learn the ropes and will help you learn to let the Bible be the light at your feet and the lamp to your path.

Let's face it; we are different than the rest of those naïve citizens out there. We see some pretty bad stuff. I have never made an actual count of all of the dead bodies that I have seen or all of the severely injured people that I have seen. I am sure the number is astronomical.

I have never kept track of how many mentally ill people that I have dealt with or how many drug addicts I have contacted in my career.

Maybe you work Narcotics. That is an eye-opening experience, I can tell you first hand. How many methamphetamine labs or drug houses have you been in? How does being in these homes affect your life?

How many kids have I seen in those meth labs? It is amazing what a set of addicted parents will allow to go on in their home just to satisfy that need. I just cannot begin to comprehend what some of the children go through who live in those homes.

Here is another heart breaker... abused kids. Man there is nothing that will make you want to lose your Jesus faster than dealing with the suspect of a child molestation or child abuse. That is a tough situation to remain objective in. I don't care what your particular field is, we all want to hurt those suspects, but we don't!

The bottom line is that sometimes our friends, family, and those around us who aren't in our chosen professions do not understand our feelings.

This section will take a Biblical look at the issues we deal with daily and what the bible says. This is not going to be an "If you're scared pray this prayer", it is more of a Bible resource on where to look when you are feeling... (Add feeling here).

It will also provide you with some scriptural relevance to the life you are going to be living and how to minister to others. I initially was going to stop this book after the initial salvation plan, but I thought better of that. God really ministered to me as I drew to a conclusion and he basically said, "Hey, dummy, your kind of people won't ask for help, so give it to them in advance". He is right. We don't normally ask for help. This will be a chance for you to learn some things on your own, without having to place the "help me" sign around your neck. No self respecting First Responder wants anyone to think they are weak right? Well, this may help you to help yourself in allowing God to help you. Make sense?

Let's get started with some basic issues first and see what God's word has to say about them.

The issues that we will be covering are the ones that I think will affect Peacekeepers and First Responders the most.

These issues that are listed will be broken down in detail in subsequent chapters of this book.

They are:

- ✓ Financial problems
- ✓ Alcohol abuse
- ✓ Depression, loneliness, Anger, and Bitterness
- ✓ Fear
- ✓ Discouragement and Disappointment
- ✓ Sinfulness

Now that I have hit every nail on the head about some the feelings and problems that you are going to face as a Christian Peace keeper, First Responder, or Corrections Officer, let me assure you that we will cover some positive things as well.

In the next few chapters, we will talk about the bad feelings that you have as a result of your job, and we will cover some of the warm and mushy stuff, too.

God gives us hope and encouragement. He even gives us enough to help us through the toughest of assignments.
If you are willing to surrender it all to him, he will give you peace in whatever situation that you find yourself in.

Don't be afraid to call out his name as he is waiting to come and be your assist car!

Chapter 9

Financial difficulties

Wow! Who hasn't had these kinds of troubles?

You are a First Responder and none of us are rich. I chose this topic first because, aside from the obvious sinful behavior that we may have participated in, this is usually the first place for fights at home.

How many remember back several chapters ago how I mentioned the boat and the truck? Yep, you guessed it. That was me. I was searching for a new outlet of happiness. In doing so, I have caused some of our most serious financial burdens ever. I didn't do this because I wanted to see what would happen.

I did this cause I was hungry for something new. I did this cause I was longing for happiness.

That may sound pretty silly, but it is true. I am not saying that you cannot have cool toys, but what I am saying is that we as First Responders are always looking for something to bless us. That blessing is always sought from things that are physical, not things that are spiritual. The spiritual things are what we are really seeking and need.

Let's take a look at what the Bible says about our financial and physical needs. If you have a bible, turn to Matthew 6:25-33.

In this passage, Jesus is addressing the needy in the town of Galilee. Jesus tells the needy not to fear or be upset about having nothing to eat or drink or having the proper clothing to wear.

Jesus tells them:

[25]"Therefore I tell you, do not be anxious about your life, what you will eat or drink, nor about your body, what you will put on it. Is not life more than food, and the body more

than clothing? [26]Look at the birds of the air: they neither sow nor reap nor gather into barns, and yet your heavenly father feeds them. Are you not of more value than they? [27] And which of you by being anxious can add a single hour to his span of life?"

[28] " And why are you anxious about clothing? Consider the lilies of the field, how they "grow: they neither toil nor spin, [29] yet I tell even Solomon in all his glory was not arrayed lie one of these. [30] But if God so clothes the grass of the field, which today is alive and tomorrow is thrown into the oven, will he not much more clothe you, O you of little faith?[31] Therefore do not be anxious, saying, 'What shall we eat?' or' What shall we drink?' or 'What shall we wear?'[32] For the Gentiles seek after all these things, and your heavenly Father knows that you need them all."

[33] " But seek first the kingdom of God and his righteousness and all these things will be added to you." (ESV)

I am no theologian, but God is trying to tell us that we should not be concerned so much with physical things. We should first concern ourselves with worshipping him and trust in him to provide for us. Don't misinterpret this by thinking that if you believe in God to provide, you don't have to do anything to help your financial situation.

God is telling us that we should always put our faith in him to provide opportunities for us when we put him first. Financial and money problems are tough and are not exclusive to our occupation. What makes them more problematic for us is that we have these problems on top of some pretty emotionally traumatic experiences.

God wants us to trust in him first and he will always provide the way for us.

Chapter 10

Alcohol Abuse

This is a touchy one for most of us. We never want to admit that you have a problem with anything. That is what makes us tough, right? Wrong. We need to know when we have problems coping with what is going on around us. That is what makes us tough.

I know that many of you will say that drinking is not a sin, and I am not saying that it is. What I am saying in this chapter is that we sometimes use booze and drugs to get us through our most trying of times.

Are you going to go to hell if you have a glass of wine with dinner? How about if you drink a couple of beers with your buddy? How about a trip to the strip club where you and your pals are going to enjoy some beers and support the local working girls? Are you going to hell now?

I don't think you are, but I do think that you are inviting problems into your life. The alcohol in it and of itself is not the problem; it is the drunkenness that is the problem.

I am saying this from experience. I was not a raging alcoholic who drank everyday. That was not my style. I didn't get drunk every weekend, nor did I drink on an every week basis. No, what I did was drink to excess when I did drink. My entire goal was to get drunk and have a good time. I will admit that I did have some good times too.

I also had some bad times. I had some times when I did not behave in accordance with God's orders. I had some times when I embarrassed my family, my office, my friends, and peers. I caused a wedge to be driven between my wife and I. Often times my drinking would result in her getting angry with me, and my drunken cop friends, and our stupid behavior. Man, it is amazing the stupid stuff grown men and women will do when they are drunk! You know what I am talking about! I can almost see a grin on your face from that last statement.

I am not proud of these behaviors. I have apologized to the people that I have hurt during those times of reckless abandon.

I can remember waking up with a HUGE headache and wondering "what the HECK did I do last night". That is not a fun experience and for those of you who have been there know exactly what I am saying.

I sometimes wondered why I was drinking to excess. Often I wondered that the next morning when I could barely move and my mouth felt like a cat had used it for a litter box. My head was throbbing and I had a guilty feeling in my heart. I think that feeling came from not completely knowing what I had did the night before. I would dread getting a telephone call from the friends that I was out with, knowing that they would be more than happy to clue me in on my foolish behavior. Man, was that a rough time in my life.

In searching my heart, I realized that what I was doing was simply being done to avoid the pain of some of the things that I have seen. It was to give me a temporary relief from whatever negative emotion that I was experiencing.

The problem was that when the effects wore off, all I had left was a headache, an angry wife, embarrassment and the same stupid problem that I had when I started.

I also realized that what I was doing was an attempt to avoid Jesus. It was an attempt to avoid doing the right thing. It was my way of covering up those empty feelings, even if it was for a little while.

Now, I said all that to say this. I am not condemning those who drink. I am not standing in the pulpit preaching fire and brimstone to those brothers and sisters who have a drink now and then; I am saying to be careful of consuming alcohol. That is what the bible says.

When you take a biblical approach to drinking, the Bible speaks out against using such substance. The Bible takes a pretty clear stance against drunkenness.

In the Book of Isaiah, Chapter 5, verse 11 speaks out against drunkenness.

It says: [11] "Woe to those who rise early in the morning, that they may run after strong drink, who tarry late into the evening as wine inflames them." (ESV)

The bible speaks about drinking in a number of places. I selected this passage of scripture because it describes what many of us may do to blow off a little steam. I say that referring to those of us who have sought refuge at the local watering hole after our tour of duty was over.

Now I am not casting stones, but I will tell you that nothing good can come from a long night of hard drinking. Although you can find references to getting drunk all through the Bible, in the Book of Ephesians, it speaks about participating in bad behavior and how we as Christians are to abstain from any form of evil.

Ephesians, Chapter 5, verse 18 says:

[18] "And do not get drunk with wine, for that is debauchery, but be filled with the spirit" (ESV)

Overall, the message that I am trying to get across to you is that by drinking, especially to excess, we invite poor behavior.

Maybe you don't prescribe to my theory, but I think that the Bible is pretty clear. It is telling us that we shouldn't get drunk or simply, when we do, we ask for trouble to come our way.

On a First Responder note, or maybe even more of a cop note; how many of us have dealt with people, who if they were sober they would not be in the situation that caused us to deal with them? Probably most of us! Alcohol increases our courage, lowers our inhibitions, and overall will help destroy our lives. We see it everyday, but most of us resort to using it as a crutch to help us through our troubled times.

Since you are a new Christian, I would urge you to cling to the Lord. Trust him to help you in troubled times. Cling to him during the storms of life. Jesus is faithful to us and will guide us in our times of need. Don't allow Satan to take away your peace by inviting him on a night out with you. Your consumption, or at least your over consumption, will allow your heart and mind to be open to all kinds of suggestions from the devil.

Who do you want in charge of your responses and your behavior, Satan or God?

Chapter 11

Depression, Loneliness, Anger and Bitterness

These are all difficult topics, but I told you in the introduction that I would make no apologies for what I say in this book.

We are very, very proud and do not like to ask for help. We don't like to ask for help with anything... ever! That is the nature of our personalities. This also holds true for when we suffer from depression and bitterness.

Many of us suffer from some form of depression, although most of us go undiagnosed. You can only see so much of this crazy stuff before you reach your breaking point.

We work long and hard at building that rough, non-emotional exterior. Never let them see you cry, right?

This is a tough job full of some of the toughest people in the world. However, inside we are crying. We are crying for the victims, crying for suspect, and crying for the families of both. Most importantly we are crying out for help for ourselves.

One of the downsides to the "JOB" is the utterly horrible things that we have to see.

Then, after it is all over and the paperwork is done, we have to go to a critical incident debriefing. Have you ever participated in one of those critical incident stress debriefings? I have and can tell you that no one, and I mean no one, ever asks for help in those. You know why? We don't ask for help during those because we are too proud and to macho to ask for help when it is being offered to us. That is just the plain and simple truth.

If you are reading this book and you're one of those counselors who conducts those, then so be it. It is the truth. I think they are wasteful and counter-productive.

If we really want to provide some emotional help for our troops then we would provide some one-on-one counseling, not a group in a semi-circle. We as First Responders aren't going to go for that. Well, maybe some will, but I don't know of many.

At this point I will not attempt to analyze you medically/mentally and will purely address this topic from a scriptural standpoint. God doesn't want us to be depressed or even bitter.

Maybe you are depressed because of failing at your marriage or relationship. Maybe you're depressed or even bitter because some moron who doesn't work as hard as you got promoted and you didn't. That is life. Get accustomed to it in this business.

It could be that you feel like the whole world is against you and that you will never get to come up for air.

Maybe you have been involved in a shooting, or seen a family parish in a house fire. It could just be that day in and day out, you see the same destructive behaviors, over and over again.

This is the life of a First Responder. We all know this and have just grown accustomed to it, but it doesn't make it any easier to deal with. We all have a breaking point that will cause us to shut down. When you reach that point who are you going to reach for to get help? Will you reach for a bottle, a pill, another person in the same boat as you are? How about reaching for God? That is what he wants you to do. Remember, he is your assist car.

You may be the toughest guy on your truck, or the meanest guy on your beat, but let me assure you that this job has gotten to you. Whether you realize it or not, it has.

It has caused countless fights at home and you may not even realize it has. It causes you to be on guard 24 hours a day, 7 days a week. You are always on watch for bad guys, or a fire, or someone who is hurt. This has an effect on you and on your family. I think this condition is called hyper-vigilance. It causes you to become cynical and bitter. It causes you to become angry and depressed. All God is asking is for you to walk with him.

God wants us to cling to him during times of depression and bitterness. As I said before, he will be faithful to you and bring you out of these times. If we take a look at Psalms, chapter 27, verses 13 and 14, we see David, King of the Jews, telling us to be strong and wait for the Lord.

[13] " I believe that I should look upon the greatness of the Lord in the land of the living! [14] Wait for the Lord; be strong and let your heart take courage; wait for the Lord" (ESV).

These verses are telling us that as believers we will be tried, yet nothing can bring us down. Through our faith comes our Christian resiliency. Keeping our eyes on God will help us from those feelings of despair and hopelessness.

The Bible also tells us that all things work out for those who believe in him. This includes any depression or bitterness that we may have.

The book of Romans 8:28 says:

[28] " And we know that for those who love God all things work together for good for those who are called according to his purpose" (ESV).

God is telling us that although we are bound to suffer in this life, those that are faithful and love him will be just fine. In this passage, God is saying to us that he will bring us out of our persecutions, afflictions, and trials.

Now I am not saying that if you go out on the town one night, drink it up, party down, and whatever else you do, there won't be consequences for your actions.

God doesn't excuse sin or negligence, but what he is saying is that for those who believe and are faithful to him, he will work out a solution that is within his own will of what should be done.

The bible also talks about being bitter.

Remember, we are Christians, right? Then why are we, as First Responders, so freaking mean to each other. You just cannot win sometimes with your co-workers. We are like a giant dysfunctional family.

We are always on each other's hind ends about anything and everything. I am just as guilty as the next guy. We are always criticizing our co-workers. Nothing they do will ever make us happy. They are always ducking calls, dodging fires, have slow responses, or they are just plain lazy.

Sometimes, we think that maybe someone we work with is getting better or more opportunities than us.

We even think that maybe we deserve more from our bosses than we are actually getting. This hurts are feelings, right? Yep I said it. I get my feelings hurt, feel cheated, feel like other people are getting something that I deserve, getting opportunities that should have been given to me. Resentment is a very nasty monster. Let's take a look at what the Bible says about resentment.

The Bible talks about a man and his sons in the parable of the prodigal son. One of his sons convinced the father to divide up his wealth and give it to them.

The younger of the two took the money and properties and basically headed into town to paint the town red.

He spent all of his money on booze and broads (no offense meant, just an old academy term).

He squandered every last dollar. The elder son was wise with his money and properties. Like always, later on in the story, the little brat ran out of money and came back. The father welcomed him with open arms and put on a huge feast for him. This angered the elder son.

Luke 15: 25-30

[25] "Now his older son was in the field, and as he came and drew near to the house, heard music and dancing. [26] And he called one of the servants and ask what these things meant. [27] And he said to him, 'Your brother has come, and your father has killed the fattened calf, because he has received him back safe and sound'. [28] But he was angry and refused to go in. His father came out and entreated him. [29]but he answered his father, 'Look, these many years I have served you and I never disobeyed your command, yet you never gave me a young goat, that I might celebrate with my friends. [30] But when this son of yours came, who has devoured your property

with prostitutes, you killed the fattened calf for him!'"(ESV)

I am not sure where you work, or exactly what Emergency Service that you work in, but I can bet you that your boss has never killed a fatted calf to celebrate your misdoings, however, that is not what this is about.

The chapter is concluded with the father's response to the elder son and I think it is fitting for us for two reasons.

[31] " And he said to him, 'Son you are always with me, and all that is mine is yours. [32]It was fitting to celebrate and be glad, for this your brother was dead, and is alive; he was lost, and is found'." (ESV)

These particular passages relates to us in a very simple manner.

First the passage is simply telling us to stop being resentful towards others. We all eventually get what is coming to us. We cannot get ourselves down by being resentful. Secondly, as Christians, we were once lost, but God didn't punish us, instead he loved us and has celebrated our return home.

I have traveled around the U.S. and visited with many other Cops, Firefighters, Paramedics, and Corrections Officers, and can tell you that it is the same everywhere. There is no paradise or Xanadu when it comes to jobs in the First Responder business.

There is always some kind of politics, back biting, stabbing in the back, end-arounds, chiefs boy/girl... you add whatever you want here! It is universal, we all are bitter about something. Maybe somebody got to ride in the front seat with the boss and you didn't. It could be as simple as your co-worker got a newer unit to drive than you did and you have more seniority. I could go on page after page with this kind of stuff, but the point I am trying to make is that we shouldn't be bitter.

God wants us to love and forgive. He doesn't want us to envy others or to be mad at them for what they receive. We should be happy with each other, not angry and fighting. Remember, we are all on THE SAME TEAM!

In Ephesians, Chapter 4, verses 31 and 32, God says for us to not be bitter. More specifically it says that we should be nice to one another. For clarification purposes, I don't necessarily think that he was specifically talking about us First Responders, but the scripture fits here.

Ephesians 4:31-32

[31] "Let all bitterness and wrath and anger and clamor and slander be put away from you, along with malice. [32] Be kind to one another, tenderhearted, forgiving one another, as God in Christ forgave you" (ESV).

Seriously? Tenderhearted? Really?

Yes, that is what God has commanded us to do. I know that it is hard. This is a very real and unforgiving world that we work and live in. Don't be bitter with your brother or sister, celebrate their opportunities and give thanks in God for you own blessings.

God knows that we, especially First Responders, will have our own trials and tribulations. He allows it and it will test our faith. We should not despair, but be thankful that God has a plan for us and that he is the mastermind behind everything.

God wants us to be happy and faithful to him. I know this is not always easy, but we must try.

When you're feeling low, depressed, or bitter, realize that God has got your back. He is your best assist car. Pray for his guidance and thank him for your blessings. Never forget to thank him for what you have because you are truly blessed whether you realize it or not.

The Bible also speaks a lot about anger and its impact on our lives. Let's take a look at the Book of Proverbs to see just what the good book says:

Proverbs 14: 29-30

[29] "Whoever is slow to anger has a great understanding, but he who has a hasty temper exalts folly. [30] A tranquil heart gives life to the flesh, but envy makes the bones rot"(ESV).

What this passage of wisdom literature is teaching us is that we should be careful about getting mad. If you are one who can control your temper and are not easily angered then you will be a patient and understanding person. If you are quick tempered then it is probably going to go very bad for you. You will probably let your temper overload your, well let's just say that you probably will write a check that your butt can't cash.

This passage isn't saying that we as Christians can never get angry. We are not perfect, but we should try and control our tempers and emotions.

The scripture goes on to talk about a "tranquil heart". What the bible is saying here is that you should try to approach all situations peacefully and in a healing manner. It also talks about envy causing the bones to rot. Huh? Really rot? Well I don't know if they are actually going to rot right there where you stand, but jealousy and anger will cause great harm to your body. They can raise you blood pressure, heart rate, and breathing rate. None of these things are good to have on a regular basis. They all take a toll on your body.

We all remember the childhood wisdom saying that "sticks and stones can break my bones but words can never hurt me", right? Well the bible talks about this very issue in regards to anger. It tells us how our angry words can cause damage to us and to others.

Before I go too much further into this subject, I encourage each of you to read the Book of Proverbs. In short, the Book of Proverbs was written by King Solomon and contains wisdom literature. Metaphorically speaking, it is the "don't put your hand on a hot stove" or "beauty is only skin deep" portion of the Bible. There is plenty of good stuff in there to help you in your everyday life. A must read. I digress, back to the book.

In Proverbs 15:1 it gives a quick look at what angry words actually do:

[1] "A soft answer turns away wrath, but a harsh word stirs up anger".

That is pretty powerful and really meaningful in this mixed up, power hungry world that we live in.

How many of us have had to do certain things at work just because our bosses said we had to? No reason, no good explanation, just do it cause I am the boss and I said so. I am not saying that bosses have to give us explanations for everything that they tell us to do. Heck, I am just happy that I have the best job in the world, but I have had to do some stuff just because "I SAID and I AM THE BOSS".

We sometimes do things in certain situations because we as First Responders become territorial, power hungry, and are trying to climb our corporate ladder so to speak. We participate in backstabbing, ladder climbing, and shin- kicking, and gossiping. What does any of this really do other than promote an angry environment?

As a Commander, I am just as guilty as the next guy in doing things because I can. There have been times, and I know you won't believe this if you have ever worked for me, that I have participated in posturing. I know, hard to believe right. I too am sometimes territorial in my duties and do not like others meddling in my business. Especially those who are not my boss and do not work for me. My peer group is who I am referring to. After all, I work hard to complete the mission that the boss wants me to complete. I don't need someone who doesn't know a thing about it trying to interfere right?

I have learned that I must stop myself from jumping the gun so to speak and to get all of the information before I react. Hopefully this approach will keep me out of trouble and keep me from foolishly opening my pie hole in an angry manner.

In the Book of Romans, God talks about what he wants us to do in regards to anger and retaliation. Now, if you are hard headed, let me assure you that this passage applies to you whether you like it or not, and NO, not everybody else that disagrees with what you do or say is a "nut job".

ROMANS 12:10-11

[10] "Love one another with brotherly affection. Outdo one another in showing

honor. [11] Do not be slothful in zeal, be fervent in spirit, serve the Lord." (ESV)

Love one another, really? Yes! God wants us to love one another and not try to outdo each other with toys or playthings. Not with rank, prestige, or money, but with honor. Yep, that's right, honor in God.

Later in the same chapter, it goes on to say that we should not be overcome by evil but that we should overcome evil deeds by doing right. The bottom line is that anger and retribution will get you kicked right in your spiritual butt. It doesn't set the example that God wants us to set and doesn't display the honorable method of life that he wants us to live.

In closing this chapter I want to talk about loneliness. I know that all of you are tough and don't ever feel alone, but I felt like I should probably mention this topic.

I sometimes feel alone so it made sense to me that I share what the Bible says about loneliness.

In 2nd Timothy, Chapter 4, verses 16-18, the Bible talks about how God was with the Apostle Paul during his imprisonment and while he awaited execution.

The passage says:

[16] "At my first defense no one came to stand by me, but all deserted me. May it not be charged against them! [17] But the Lord stood by me and strengthened me, so that through me the message might be fully proclaimed and all the Gentiles might hear it. So I was rescued from the lion's mouth. [18] The Lord will rescue me from every evil deed and bring me safely into his heavenly kingdom. To him be the glory forever and ever. Amen." (ESV)

This passage is referring to a man who was awaiting execution for preaching the word of God.

In this passage, he is instructing his son, Timothy, to keep the faith and continue preaching the message.

God will never leave us nor forsake us. He is always with us and awaiting our cry for help.

Additionally, the Bible talks about loneliness in Hebrews, Chapter 12:6;

[5] "...I will never leave you nor forsake you"(ESV)

Although we sometimes feel lonely, we should always be aware that God is with us and we are never alone.

All you have to do in times of trouble, times of loneliness, and times of despair is to call out his name. God is always with us. He is there to be your ultimate back up.

Chapter 12

Fear

I realize from my own personal experiences that most of us never are scared of anything. So reading this chapter may come as a boring proposition to you, but go ahead and read it. After all, you might be able to share what the Bible has to say about fear with someone who isn't as tough as you.

So please, go ahead and read it, that way when you do get one of those "scared of their own shadow" partners, you can help them out.

As I stated earlier, we live in a very real and violent world. We deal with some of the meanest gang members, hottest fires, and worst working conditions around. We find ourselves in slums, jail cells, roach infested mobile homes, flop houses, drug houses, and so on and so forth.

If the violent people and their poor choices of behavior don't scare the devil right out of you, the filth should.

We live in a world full of violent, deranged people. These are people who suffer from mental illness, drug induced sickness, blood borne diseases, environmental hazards, and criminal behavior.

These people conduct their lives outside the established social and biblical norms that were established years ago.

They are people, who due to misfortune or poor decision making skill, have came into contact with a Peace Keeper or First Responder. These are the basic drunks, drug addicts, needle freaks, meth heads, pill poppers, scum bags, bullies, and loud mouths.

These people are generally emotionally driven and alcohol or drug fueled. You never know how each encounter with them is going to turn out. You might have dealt with a meth head a hundred times in the past and they were always cooperative. Then, you deal with them on the one hundred and first time and it might be the one where they decide that they are not going to jail and they will do whatever it takes to keep you from taking them.

It could be the third fire call of the day and its only a kitchen fire. You have handled a thousand of those in your career. This one might be different. Maybe the fire was set intentionally to draw Emergency personnel in so that someone could ambush them. You just never know what is around the corner, do you?

We both know that our jobs are dangerous and it is ok to be fearful. Fear oftentimes results in our own heroic actions. A good healthy dose of fear helps as long as we do not allow it to control us. If we allow fear to control our actions, we will allow fear and the devil to win.

There were many brave men and women in the Bible. Their faith was tested and tried. These men and women all had fear but the one common denominator was that they didn't allow the fear to overcome them.

Have you ever thought about being thrown into a Lion's Den? Personally I would like to pet a lion but only under controlled conditions, but I digress. Seriously, think about that.

Imagine reporting to duty one day and your boss mad at you. You have failed to complete a task that your boss told you to get done. The next thing you know, the boss is throwing you into a hole, filled with hungry, vicious, and angry Lions.

They throw you in and lock the door behind you, leaving you alone to become dinner for these beasts. Sound scary? I know that I would probably soil myself and cry for my mom, but that is just me. This very story happened in the Bible.

In brief, Daniel, a young man in Jerusalem, was taken as a servant during King Nebuchadnezzar's siege of Jerusalem.

It seems that King Nebuchadnezzar, the ruler of Babylon, took many of the most intelligent and strapping young men of Jerusalem into his service during his siege of the Holy City. In doing so, he would train them in Babylonian ways, language, and most of all worship.

Daniel, who would later have his name changed to Belteshazzar, would serve this king as a political advisor and dream interpreter of sorts.

To shorten this story for now, Daniel chose continue praying to God as he had always done, instead of worshiping the King as he had been directed in the Kings edict. Several little snitches came and told on Daniel and the King was forced to take action. The King summoned for Daniel and when Daniel admitted to the violation of the edict, the King was forced to carry out the deadly discipline. King Nebuchadnezzar didn't want to throw Daniel into the Lion's Den, but because of his own edict, he was forced to do so. If he didn't throw Daniel into the Lion's Den, the all of his other edicts would be disobeyed and no one would honor his rules that he makes.

In Daniel, Chapter 6:16-18, the King throws Daniel into the Den and tells him:

[16] "... 'May your God, whom you serve continually, deliver you." (ESV)

In passage seventeen, the King has a large stone placed over the mouth of Lion's Den and then seals it with his ring. (This is a custom of kings all through the centuries. It is much like our own signature now)

After a sleepless night the King went back to the Lion's Den to check on Daniel. The King liked Daniel and thought highly of him. We he went to the den he called out to Daniel, knowing and expecting that Daniel was dead. He knew that Daniel had been devoured by the Lion's but hoped that Daniel's God had rescued him. The King was doubtful but wanted to check for himself. When he arrived at the Lion's Den he called out to Daniel.

Daniel 6:20-22

[20] "As he came near to the den where Daniel was, he cried out in a tone of anguish. The King declared to Daniel, "Oh Daniel, servant of the living God, has your God, whom you serve continually, been able to deliver you from the lions?" [21] Then Daniel said to the king, "Oh King live forever! [22] My God sent his angel and shut the lion's mouths, and they have not harmed me, because I was found blameless before him; and also before you, O king, I have done no harm". (ESV)

Although this is an abbreviation of the story, the central theme here is to trust in God. To trust him to deliver you from all harm.

Daniel held fast to his faith in God and God sent an angel to shut the lion's mouths and kept them from killing and devouring Daniel.

I don't know about you but I have never faced the possibility of being thrown into a Lion's Den, but I have had my share of risky situations. All of us have had them. We have all been in dangerous situations and faced down some pretty nasty foes. If you spend any time on the job you will be called to face some pretty rough incidents and enemies. That is the hard truth of this business.

The Bible talks a lot about fear. Let's take a look at another passages concerning fear:

Psalms 16:8

[8] " I have set the Lord always before me; because he is at my right hand, I shall not be shaken". (ESV)

You and me, we have to put the Lord in charge of our lives. He is going to protect us.

We have to put him right there in front of our pistols, axes, fire houses, restraint chairs, pepper spray, batons, flash bangs, ballistic shield, and every other tool that we use to protect us. When we have faith in him to protect and guide us, there is no reason to fear anything or any man.

I know that no one who read this chapter is afraid of anything, but please take the message and help out your brother or sister. They do get scared.

Remember, God is your only real assist car.

Chapter 13

Discouragement and disappointment

I have already covered a lot of this when I talked about Bitter and Anger, but let's face the facts; we do suffer from a lot of discouragement and disappointment.

These Police, Fire, EMS, and Corrections jobs are not for the faint of heart. We have got to put up with some of the most difficult individuals in the weirdest situations ever.

Just for fun, how many civilians have ever watched someone write a letter on a jail wall with their own feces? How many civilians have ever seen the aftermath of a plane crash? How many have ever watched someone die while their family looks on, yelling for you to do something?

This is the stuff that the regular people out there don't get to see. They get to live their lives blissfully ignorant while we see all of the bad stuff going on around us.

I said all that to say this, we see all kinds of bad stuff everyday and it leads to us having a bad taste in our mouth for people. This all has a profound effect on our level of peace.

Ok, so let's us put this into perspective. We see the worst of people during the lowest points in their lives. Then, to add insult to injury, we suffer career and personal disappointments.

How about the time when you deserved the promotion and some other knucklehead who doesn't work as hard as you got it? Why did they get it? Well the devil will probably tell you it is because they are the bosses buddy. The devil knows that you are already mad about some of the derelict people that you have to deal with, and now, somebody else gets promoted ahead of you. How about your agency hiring someone and putting them right into a position that they haven't earned? Maybe this is a position that you have wanted for years. You wanted it, but POOF, it is given to some rookie who just started a couple of minutes ago. Will that make you mad? Needless to say, it probably will.

Let's take a turn for some personal stuff. How about if your kid gets arrested for an arson? Front page news? I would think so. The headline will probably read...

"(COPS, FIREFIGHTERS, EMS, CORRECTIONS OFFICERS) kid arrested for burning down the local
_____!"

If you are a First Responder of any kind, I will almost bet that the news headline will mention something about your kid being the child of a First Responder. It is all part of the job. The news media sensationalizes everything. One of our kids does something stupid and it is now news.

This hasn't happened to me, but it could. Would I be disappointed? You bet I would. I have raised my children to be good, solid, smart thinking young people. I would be very disappointed if they participated in something like that.

How about if your spouse is diagnosed with cancer? Disappointing and discouraging? To say the least! How about if your spouse is cheating on you? Even worse, how about if it is with someone you work with? Disappointing and discouraging? On this one you might want to refer back to the anger chapters, but the point I am trying to make is that we all suffer disappointment and discouragement.

Maybe you try really hard at work but seem to be getting nowhere in seeking a promotion. Maybe everyone seems to be getting the upper hand on you. Your career or marriage is stagnant and you just feel like no matter what you do, nothing is going to help.

Well, here is the help that you need. You can find that help in God's word.

Galations 6:9-10

[9] "And let us not grow weary of doing good, for in due season we will reap, if we do not give up. [10] So then, as we have opportunity, let us do good to everyone, and especially to those who are of the household of faith". (ESV)

God is telling us to be patient and that good things will come to those of us who are willing to continue working. We can never give up because God is with us and he is on our side.

I am not saying that God is going to give you everything that you pray for or want. God has a plan for all of us. We don't know it and no one besides God knows what that plan is. God will give us what he wants us to have, but we must continue to work at what we want.

You also have to spiritualize this in the context that we serve God. We must continue to work diligently in serving him if we want to reach the prize on the other side. That prize is Heaven. That prize is eternal life.

That prize is a life free from discouragement and disappointment.

So now, when you are completely filled with disappointment and are so discouraged that you just don't know where to turn, take a look towards God. He is pretty amazing stuff. He will give you that peace to help you through life's little disappointments.

Matthew 11:28-30

[28] "Come to me, all who labor and are heavy laden, and I will give you rest. [29] Take my yoke upon you, and learn from me, for I am gentle and lowly in heart, and you will find rest for your souls. [30] For my yoke is easy, and my burden light". (ESV)

God understands that we will get discouraged. He understands that we will get mad, upset, disappointed, and all of those other things. After all, we are sinners.

We must turn to him at all times and especially during times of discouragement and disappointment. It is the only way we can make it through these times in one piece.

God wants to help us through these times and through all of our times. He wants to be our back up car. Pick up your spiritual walkie-talkie and give him a yell. He will come to your aid.

Chapter 14

Sinfulness

This chapter is going to cover some scriptural information about sin. I am not going to get into the "what is a sin" topic with anyone.

What I do know is a sin, for sure, is worshipping anything other than God. This could be worshipping your truck, your job, your spouse, an activity, or anything else that would detract from serving him. This I know for sure.

Rather than make a list of what I think are sins, let's take a look at it from a wisdom standpoint.

First, let us take a look in the Book of Psalms.

Psalms 1: 1-6

[1] "Blessed is the man who walks not in the counsel of the wicked, nor stands in the way of sinners, nor sits in the seats of scoffers; [2] but his delight is in the law of the Lord, and on his law he mediates day and night. [3] He is like a tree planted by streams of water that yields its fruit in its season, and its leaf does not wither. In all that he does, he prospers. [4] The wicked are not so, but are like chaff that the wind drives away. [5] Therefore the wicked will not stand in the judgment, nor sinner in the congregation of the righteous; [6] for the Lord knows the way of the righteous, but the way of the wicked will perish". (ESV)

This passage, in a nutshell, is telling us to walk in the manner that God has told us to walk. It is all in the bible, every situation, every commandment, it is all in there. We have to search his word to find what is sinful.

The bottom line, based on this passage is that in order for us to gain heaven, we must walk in his ways. The Lord knows that we are sinful. Adam and Eve messed the whole thing up in the beginning, but we must press on. Live by his ways or die by your own is the bottom line.

We have to be careful who we associate with and how we behave. Have you ever heard the saying "If it walks like a duck, quacks like a duck, and has a bill like a duck, then it probably is a duck"? Well that is kind of what God is saying here in Psalms 1.

He is telling us to stick by him and to not associate with non-believers. I don't mean that you cannot go to your agency functions or parties. You can be a shining light for those people as long as you behave based on your convictions, beliefs, and Gods word. Otherwise, you are just going to be one of them.

In 1 John, 1:7-10

[7] " But if we walk in the light, as he is in the light, we have fellowship with one another and the blood of Jesus his Son cleanses us from all

sin. [8] If we say we have no sin, we deceive ourselves, and the truth is not in us. [9] If we confess our sins, he is faithful and just to forgive us our sins and to cleanse us from all unrighteousness. [10] If we say we have not sinned, we make him a liar, and his word is not in us." (ESV)

The bottom line is simply this; Sin is anything that takes you away from worshiping God. This can be anything. It could be something as simple as a boat, or as minor as hanging out with people who aren't Christians. As First Responders we are typically held to a higher standard of behavior than civilians, right? God is the same way. He holds his children to a higher level of behavior than he expects from those who refuse a personal relationship with him.

Keep your head high and do the right things. Do the things that God wants you to do, the right things.

Chapter 15

"Respectfully submitted"

As we near the end of this book, I pray that it was an inspiration to you. I hope that it will minister to your soul and help shape you into the Christian Warrior that God intended you to be.

Our jobs are difficult. They just don't make easy First Responder jobs no matter what discipline you are in. The way in which you handle the stresses of the job will impact your life. God wants to help you through these stresses. He wants to be the lighthouse on the shore and the port in the storm.

I challenge each of you to make a covenant with God and be a faithful servant to him. I can assure you that God has given me a great peace in my life. If he can do it for me, I know that he will do it for you as well.

To close it off, I want to give you a few more scriptures that may help you put some of our duties into perspective.

<u>Deuteronomy 16:20</u>

[20] "Justice, and only justice, you shall follow, that you may live and inherit the land that the Lord your God is giving you." (ESV)

<u>Psalms 20:1</u>

[1] "May the Lord answer you in the day of trouble" May the name of the God of Jacob protect
you!

<u>Psalms 82:4</u>

[4] "Rescue the weak and needy; deliver them from the hand of the wicked."

There are a lot of scriptural references to our jobs in the Bible. Too many to list here and I hope that through your faithful service to God that you will spend some time reading his good book.

Take some time to pray every day. Trust that God will provide comfort and protection to you and your family. Read the Bible and attend church regularly. Make friendships with Christians and spend time with them learning about God's mercy and grace.

I know that you will feel much better walking with God than you did when you were running from him.

We all have a higher calling than just public service. We have a calling to serve God and be a light to the world. Don't miss your opportunity to shine your Christian light bar so that all can see. May God wrap his protective hands around you and bless you with wisdom and strength. Thank you for your service to your community and to your chosen profession.

After all,

God wants to be your assist car!

About the Author:

Tommy is an 18 year veteran of a large Sheriff's Office in the State of Missouri. He has served as a Road Deputy, Jail Commander, Chief of Detectives, and Tactical Team Officer/Leader. He has worked in Undercover Narcotics, and later led one of the most successful Narcotics/Meth-Lab interdiction teams in the United States.

He is a husband, father of two, and a new Christian for the SECOND TIME IN HIS LIFE.

Growing up in church, Tommy learned the basics about God and living a Christ like life. He strayed away after being on the "Job" for a number of years. He is now back with God and ready for action!

Made in the USA
Charleston, SC
28 November 2010